she dreams when she bleeds

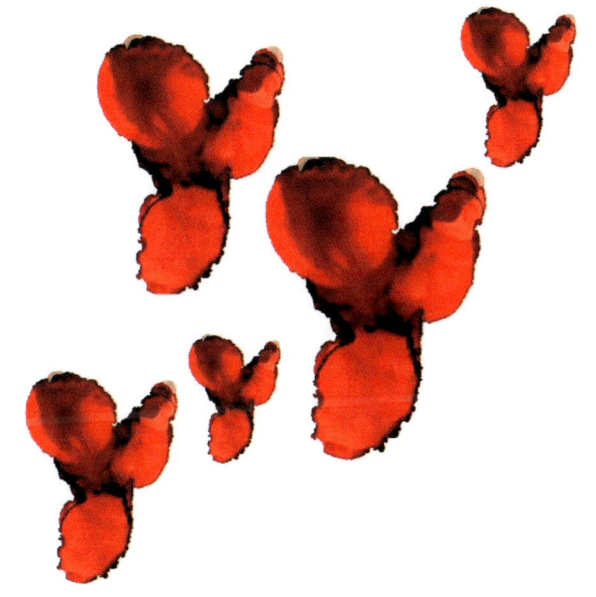

She Dreams
When She Bleeds

poems about periods

NIKKI TAJIRI

Copyright © 2019 by Nikki Tajiri

All rights reserved. No part of this book may be used or reproduced in any manner whatsoever without written permission except in the case of reprints in the context of reviews.

Printed by Kindle Direct Publishing in the United States of America
Illustrations and design by Nikki Tajiri

First printing, 2019

Published by Nikki Tajiri
Instagram @nikkitajiri
Email nik.tajiri@gmail.com

To Zoe

And to all our newest menstruators

nikki tajiri

Today is the day
Not an ordinary day
Where are the trumpets
Where are the cameras

Today is the day
First blood
Shed your old skin
Shed your old self

Today is the day
A new energy arises in you
It is time to celebrate
It is time to menstruate

she dreams when she bleeds

Did you think you could control me
Ignore me
Walk all over me
Separate yourself from me
I am you and you are me

My wish
Is that my daughter looks forward to her first bleed
That she knows it is a special, sacred, beautiful event
To be celebrated like the day of her birth

I know
In order for her to love her first blood
She must see me loving mine
She must see her father treating her mother like gold while menstruating
She must hear women saying it is good and we are proud

she dreams when she bleeds

Our monthly blood is
The divine feminine
Wild and messy and
In need of nurturing one moment
And roaring power the next

Connecting us to our women
Our tribe our sisters
A connection that needs no words

Our grandmother's grandmother
Had the same blood flowing
You are being called back
To your body again

If women used to cycle with the moon
Did we all used to be in sync
Keeping the world's rhythm inside ourselves

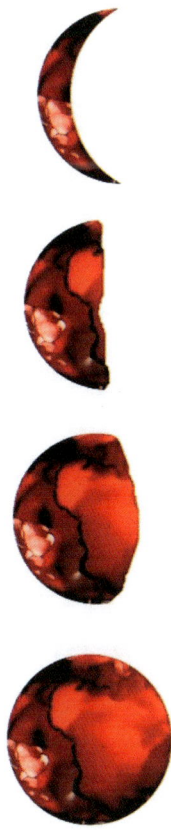

she dreams when she bleeds

To my younger self
Your period is a gift and not a curse
It's not easy to explain
But now I wouldn't trade it away for all the money in the world

One day you will look forward to bleeding
And you will appreciate the magic in the cycle
And you will wish you could go back to the first time you bled
And listen to what your body was saying back then

One day your periods will stop
And your body will protest against the abuse
You will shriek with joy when it comes again after a year of waiting

One day you will have a daughter
And she will light up your world
Like never before
And you will pray with all your might that she will have a different relationship with her period than you had

Stop
No longer will I
Keep calm and carry on while I bleed
I refuse to ignore this any longer

A wounded warrior would
Not continue to hunt
Unless it was urgently needed

Goddesses dream when they bleed
And I don't want to miss
Any more

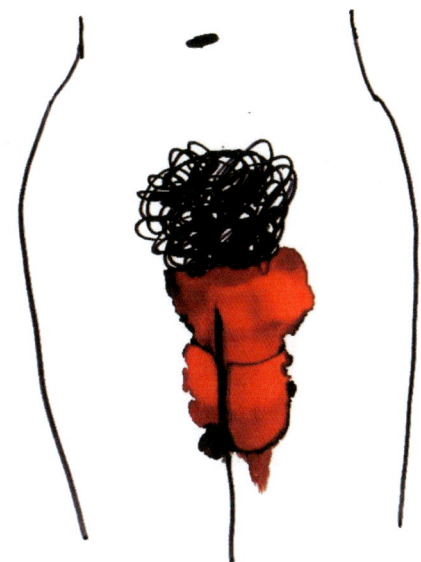

The truth is that
I cannot love being a women
While hating my period

To the men
Who call periods gross
Is it also gross that you started your life in your
mother's womb
Nourished by her blood
Is it gross that at the moment of your birth
You came out screaming and covered in her blood
Freshly unwrapped from the organ your mother
grew from nothing
Is it gross that one day your daughter will bleed

What is gross is that your attitude
Will make your daughter wish she was
Born a boy

she dreams when she bleeds

Men have shed blood in battle
But all the blood they have shed is nothing
Compared to the women of the world

The years I was on the pill
Was a decade lost
Feeling lost
Unanchored
Emotions dulled
Not myself
I thought it was just a side effect of becoming an adult

I've lost complete faith
In doctors who told me
That synthetic hormones are totally fine
That they are equal to the real thing
That there are no downsides
Typical human arrogance
Typical masculine rationality
Young women, beware

she dreams when she bleeds

Sometimes our bodies can be honest
In a way our minds cannot

It's a new red tent
It's one built by women for themselves
To dream to laugh to cry
To sit and be
To honor all that it means to be a woman

She will emerge when she is ready
And men beware
Any snarky word or condescending comment
Any smear on the red tent
Will bring the wrath of her sisters

Trained and encouraged
To ignore it
Push through it
Suppress it

Pretend nothing is happening
Do not complain
Do not make a mess
Do not be a burden

Be happy and kind even if you don't feel like it
Finish your work even if you don't feel like it
Look presentable even if you don't feel like it
Pop a pill and keep going

What violence is this
What nonsense
I'm sorry for all the times I have said this
To myself

nikki tajiri

The first time I bled I must have been eleven
The only feeling I remember was relief
Because I had spent years
Dreading and worrying and fearing

I told my mom and I think she said yay
Other than that it was a non-event
Not marked in any way
Just the start of a monthly burden

This month I will celebrate for my eleven year old self
I will pour my blood on the earth and
I will buy myself red flowers and
I will go to the ocean and spend time with myself

Congratulations to you young woman, young warrior
For your journey has just begun

she dreams when she bleeds

Men
You may never understand what it's like to bleed
To have your insides streaming out of you
Like a chocolate bar melting on a sidewalk
To have the walls to your very being become thinner

You may never understand what it's like to be shamed
For something so innate to you
It's like shaming men for semen coming out of their bodies
They would never stand for it

You may never understand completely what a period is like
But it helps to try

nikki tajiri

This is the first time in a long time
Where I will allow my blood to flow out
I have always plugged it with tampons or cups
Thinking what is the difference

But as the blood trickles out
It demands attention
It demands to be felt, seen, smelt
It demands me to be here

And now I wonder if I will ever go back to
containing
What is the difference
It is the difference between a river
And a dam

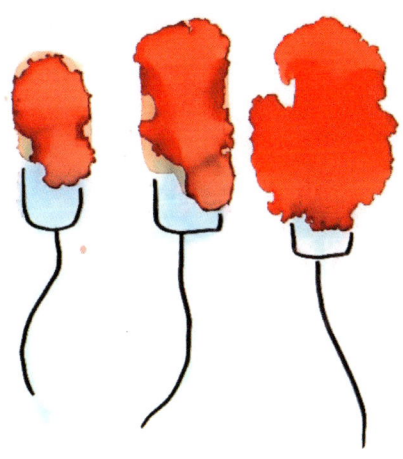

How am I beautiful
When I am pregnant
But not when I am menstruating

Don't you know
You can't have one
Without the other

nikki tajiri

Her blood is not refuse or excrement
Even though she flushes it and washes it away
Her blood is lava flowing
Her blood is holy water
Her blood is gold

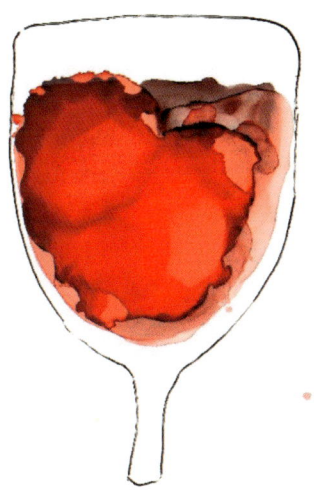

she dreams when she bleeds

I imagine one day you will want boys to like you
And you will do what women have done since the
beginning of time
And hide the parts of yourself they won't like
But here's the rub

Most boys will never like your period
Most will never admit they are scared of the blood
For them blood only comes with injury and death
With conflict and violence

They cannot understand a blood that comes in communion
A friendly blood that visits every month for decades
A vibrant blood that means you are healthy and fertile
A bonding blood that moves you closer to your tribe

Some boys will be jealous
When you give your body time and space and tender care
When you focus on yourself instead of on them
They do not have a body clock like yours

But I hope you find a man
Who embraces all of who you are
Who falls into rhythm with you
And loves you for your blood instead of
In spite of it

nikki tajiri

No one else sees it
No one else wants to
Only she can see
The beauty in her blood

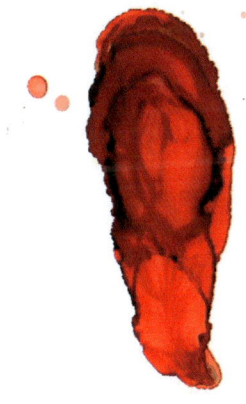

There are different ways to fall in love with your blood
One day it might hit you like a slap in the face
A mind blown wtf revelation
That's the way it happened for me

Or it might be a slower process
Where you really get to know each other
Gathering information and trust
And after a while it occurs to you that you might be in love

What if we all fell in love
With our bodies and our hormones and our periods
With our cyclical natures and our ups and our downs
That kind of love could change the world

nikki tajiri

Oh you don't want to talk about periods
Well there are 3.8 billion women here on this earth
right now
Who might disagree
Yes 3,800,000,000 women
They might find this conversation relevant
Oh and out of those women I bet at least
eight hundred million
Are bleeding as we speak
Yes 800,000,000 women
Bleeding together
We will drown you in our blood

The number 800,000,000 comes from Anna Dahlqvist's book, *It's Only Blood: Shattering the Taboo of Menstruation*. London: Zed Books, 2018, 177.

she dreams when she bleeds

I wish I was much gentler and kinder
To other women on their periods

I wish I never said a harsh word
About how or where they bled

I wish I held more space for them
And helped them more
Even if they didn't ask

I wish I stood up in defense
When I heard a man spouting hate towards her period
I wish I corrected his perspective

But don't you know
Period wishes only come true
If you tell everyone you know

Even if you don't think your blood is beautiful
Can you appreciate the complexity
The symphony that is our hormones
Your whole body coded into every single cell

Can you appreciate the symmetry
Left ovary right ovary left ovary right ovary
The egg rolling down that red carpet

Can you appreciate the rhythm
The millions of blood cells falling away
Then rebuilding over again
The faithful repetition month in and month out

Even if you don't think your blood is beautiful
Can you appreciate it all the same

After forty years of bleeding
I don't want to look back and think
About pain and shame
About hiding and cleaning
I'm done with negativity

After forty years of bleeding
I want to have fond memories and nostalgia for those
Times of reflection and introspection
Times of stillness and space
Period positive

nikki tajiri

Our period is the ocean tide
That smooths the sand
And rises with the moon

It is the heavy rain
That swells the rivers
And washes away debris

It is a glacial waterfall
That flows in the summer
And freezes in the winter

Our period is a microcosm
Of the earth herself
You have a whole world inside of you

she dreams when she bleeds

Halfway done
Twenty years of bleeding behind me
I make this sacred vow to myself
The next twenty years of bleeding
Will look completely different

Can I accept my period for what it is
Can I accept myself for who I am

Can I accept that my period will never be perfect
Can I accept that I will never be perfect

Can I accept that my period is cyclical and not linear
Can I accept that my life is cyclical and not linear

Can I accept that my period might have deeper
meaning
Can I accept that my life might have deeper
meaning

Maybe if I can accept my period without judgment
Then I can accept myself without judgment

I have probably bled over two hundred times
One thousand days and nights
And this time feels like the first time

For the first time I am bleeding with the New Moon
Like the first women did

For the first time I consider my period a dear friend
Instead of an unwelcome houseguest

For the first time I let my blood wash into the ocean
This period is one I'll never forget

nikki tajiri

Every woman you know and love
Every woman you admire from afar
Every frenemy and foe
Chances are you've bled together

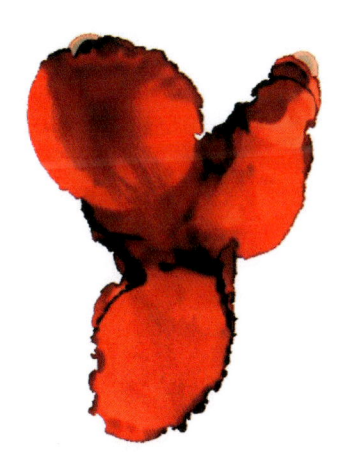

He looked and he wondered
How she could bleed so much
And emerge so strong

I can imagine a world
Where periods are loved

Where we eagerly anticipate
The ideas and inspiration
Gathered from them

Where we expect the break
Like a weekend retreat
Or an annual vacation

Where we talk about them
With affection and warmth

Where we set up our world
To accommodate
And support them

I can imagine a world
Where it feels so good to bleed

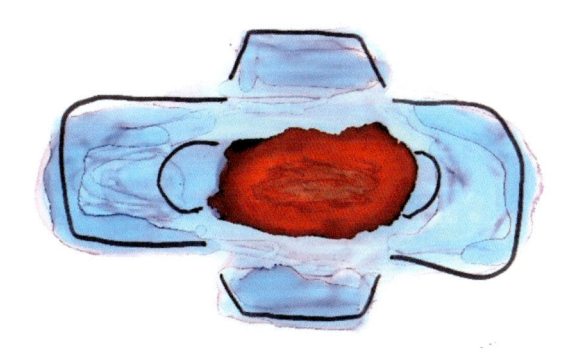

I'm still learning to love my blood
It's hard
The blood and the mucus and the clots
The cramps
The smell
My first reaction isn't love

My love starts small
Appreciating flashes of red
Swirls in water
Noticing and surrendering
Slowing

A new intimacy
This will take time

nikki tajiri

Now I see a red lip
And I can't help but smile

Why do I feel the need to
Read a gynecology textbook
To legitimize my experience

As if I need to know
Everything about my anatomy
In order to feel it

We can name
Every single body part
We can list
All the things that can go wrong

Does all that naming and listing
Really inspire respect or awe or gratitude or wisdom
Or does it just
Separate us further

nikki tajiri

I want you to know that however you bleed is beautiful
Whether it is a gush or a trickle
Whether you use a tampon or a pad or a cup
Whether you bleed through your clothes
Or all over your bed

However you bleed is beautiful
Whether it is out in nature or at your desk
Whether it is by yourself
Or surrounded by people

However you bleed is beautiful
Whether it is an angry bleed or a joyful bleed
Whether it is a tearful bleed
Or a bleed where you don't feel much of anything

However you bleed is beautiful
I hope one day
You will think so too

she dreams when she bleeds

Talking and laughing
We strolled into the house after dinner with your dad
And then we all saw it at the same time
And there was a pause

Your dog took my bloody pads
Out of the bathroom garbage
Chewed them up
And scattered them all over the house
And your dad had no idea what they were

And you didn't really know either
Because I was the first one to get my period
And we hadn't talked about it yet

You recovered first
I remember so clearly although 20 years have passed
You said
Oh I know, I'll clean it up, don't worry about it Dad
And your dad was the awkward guy that he was

And I sat with him with the TV on
More ashamed than I had ever been
Hating myself and my body and my period

And all I want to do is to go to that girl
And hold her and comfort her
And convince her that she did nothing wrong
And share stories until her shame becomes sisterhood

If there is one thing we can count on
In menstruation and in life
It is unpredictable

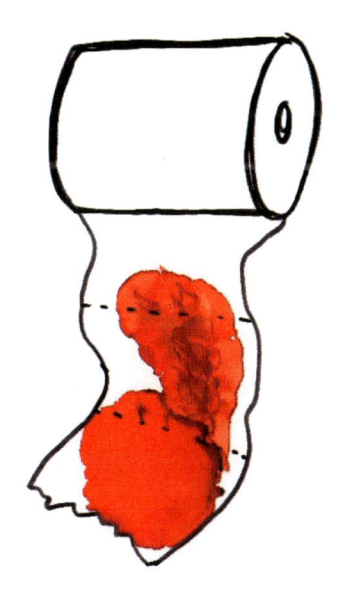

she dreams when she bleeds

I am beyond blessed
To be surrounded by baby girls

It breaks my heart to think that one day
Even for a moment
They will feel like they are not enough
Because of their blood

It breaks my heart to think
That most women will never uncover the power and beauty of their periods
That most women will despise their blood until the moment it stops

It breaks my heart to think
That most women are told their blood is unclean
That most women have period shame seeped deep into their bones

Let's bleed out loud
For our daughters

nikki tajiri

Is it just biology
Sex is just biology
Emotions are just biology
Childbirth is just biology
Menstruation is just biology

Maybe our first mistake
Was when we tried to tell everyone
That it was just biology

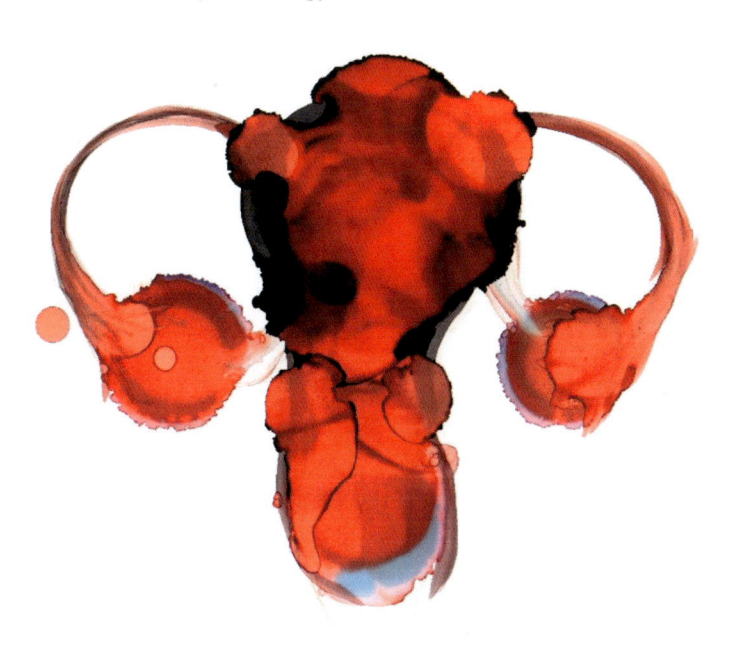

she dreams when she bleeds

I'm walking into my time now
My dreams are bright movies
Clutter is making me antsy
Demands have me on edge
I could love being alone forever
Here we go

You might tell me that your period causes you pain
So much pain that it consumes your life
How can you love your period through pain like this

There are not enough words to tell you
How resilient and courageous you are
And I don't know what will happen
But out of everyone that could process that pain
I trust you with it the most

she dreams when she bleeds

So you think that
Because you do not menstruate
It has nothing to do with you

But what if your life is
Regulated by all the women around you
Without you even knowing it

And what if she has the intuition
And wisdom we seek
During those uninterrupted bleeds

And what if you could be better
At supporting someone that you love

Maybe there is no such thing as
Nothing to do with me
Anymore

Although I may bleed with the moon
When I bleed I am the sun
With all its rays pointed inwards
And everything around me sucked in by my gravity
All the treasure all the garbage

A vortex
Drinking it in
Bleeding it out

she dreams when she bleeds

Trying to rush through a bleed
Is like trying to rush autumn
Or like trying to tell rain to fall faster
It cannot be rushed

One day I tried to tell myself
I didn't have time to bleed
If I have time to breathe
Then I have time to bleed

Choose scarcity and negativity
Too much blood
Too much time wasted
Too much cramping
Too much emotion

Or choose abundance and gratitude
Abundant blood
Abundant rest
Abundant sensation
Abundant introspection

Dearest body
Dearest self
Thank you

she dreams when she bleeds

Of course I'm allowed to feel different throughout
my cycle
Sometimes I feel a thousand different ways in a
single day, hour, minute
Does anyone feel the same in the height of summer
and the dead of winter

I'm now starting to notice
The climbing and blooming
And then the cloaking and nesting
Spring summer autumn winter

I guess I'm not crazy
I'm just cyclical

They poisoned us
And then
They trained us to fear our own blood
A biohazard
Contaminated

No
I will not fear my body
I will not reject part of myself

I am whole
I am safe
I am free

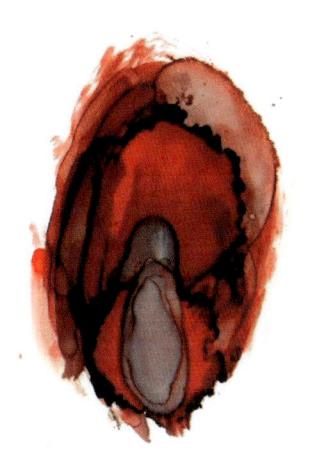

she dreams when she bleeds

For all of our newcomers
It might be hard to tell
Your friends about your period

But let me tell you
About the bond you will feel
When someone says
Me too

Notes to self on having a great bleed
Do whatever you want
Wait turn off your phone
Now do whatever you want

Stay away from stressed out people
Keep warm
Drink tea in your favorite cup
Go outside and stare at the trees and the sky
Do nothing for a while

The to-do list can wait
Other people can wait
Bleed on

she dreams when she bleeds

No one outright says it
That we shouldn't listen to our bodies
That we should ignore our natural rhythms
But here is how it happens

First we go to school as a child
And then we can't eat when we want to
Or use the toilet when we want to
We can't take days off when we want to
We get accustomed to ignoring our bodies

And then we get our periods
And our lives get busier
I can't miss that exam
I can't miss that soccer game
I can't miss work
Having your period is not a good excuse

And the tampon companies told me
That I should not have to miss out
Because I am leak proof
And this tampon is the one for active girls

And now I don't even know how
To listen to my body
It's been decades since I have actually let my body
lead the way

And maybe the doctor can help decode
Because now my body hates me
And my period hates me

Your period doesn't hate you
It just wants to talk

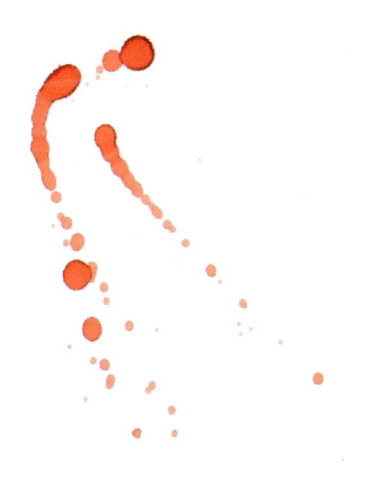

she dreams when she bleeds

This wasn't the journey I imagined
But it was the journey I needed
I started this for my daughter
But it ended up being for myself
Healing the scars I couldn't see

I trust my body and
I trust my period
To lead me home

nikki tajiri

We are not finished
Discussing menstruation
Telling our stories of menstruation
Elevating our menstruation
We have not even started

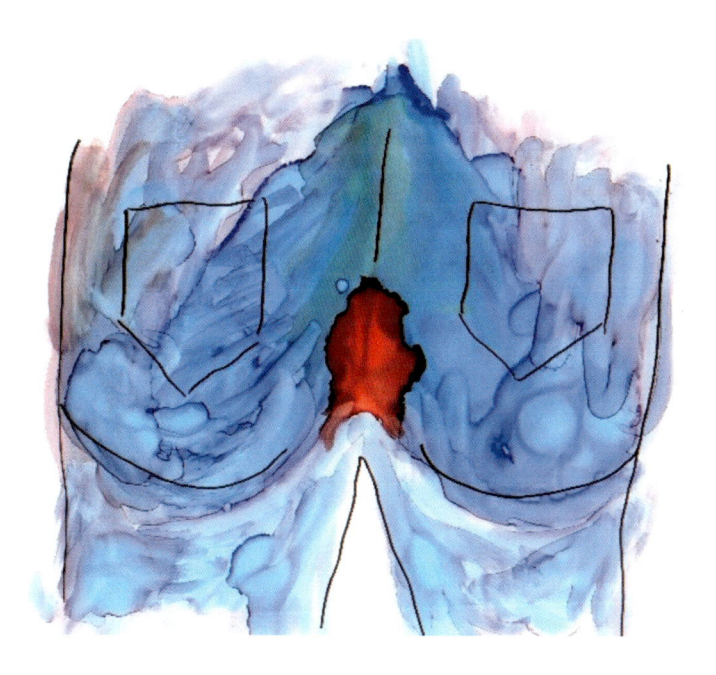

Note to the Reader

Hello Beautiful Reader,

I hope this work helps heal you as it helped to heal me. I hope this works helps you to love and accept yourself a little bit deeper. I hope this work shifted your perspective.

I encourage you to revisit here from time to time. These writings and artwork were done at all different times in my cycle. How I feel when I reflect back on them changes constantly, depending on who I am in that moment.

I think now we are all realizing how fluid gender is and I love that. As has been so lovingly pointed out to me, not everyone who menstruates is a woman, and not all women menstruate. These writings might not reflect your experience and that's okay too. It's just one perspective of millions.

Sending you so much love and peace wherever you are,

Nikki

About the Author

Nikki
She is a mother,
A poet,
An artist.
She is a homebody,
A book lover,
Plant eater.
When she laughs it echoes down every hallway,
She was raised near mountains and carries them in her heart.

Photo: Rebekah Paul Photography